DISCOVERING DINOSAURS

Diplodocus

Kimberley Jane Pryor

Marshall Cavendish
Benchmark
New York

This edition first published in 2012 in the United States of America by Marshall Cavendish Benchmark
An imprint of Marshall Cavendish Corporation

This publication represents the opinions and views of the author based on Kimberley Jane Pryor's personal experience, knowledge, and research. The information in this book serves as a general guide only. The author and publisher have used their best efforts in preparing this book and disclaim liability rising directly and indirectly from the use and application of this book.

Other Marshall Cavendish Offices:
Marshall Cavendish International (Asia) Private Limited, 1 New Industrial Road, Singapore 536196 • Marshall Cavendish International (Thailand) Co Ltd. 253 Asoke, 12th Flr, Sukhumvit 21 Road, Klongtoey Nua, Wattana, Bangkok 10110, Thailand • Marshall Cavendish (Malaysia) Sdn Bhd, Times Subang, Lot 46, Subang Hi-Tech Industrial Park, Batu Tiga, 40000 Shah Alam, Selangor Darul Ehsan, Malaysia

Marshall Cavendish is a trademark of Times Publishing Limited

Library of Congress Cataloging-in-Publication Data

Pryor, Kimberley Jane.
  Diplodocus / Kimberley Jane Pryor.
     p. cm. — (Discovering Dinosaurs)
  Summary: "Discusses the physical characteristics, time period, diet, and habitat of the Diplodocus" —Provided by publisher.
  Includes bibliographical references and index.
  ISBN 978-1-60870-536-8
  1. Diplodocus—Juvenile literature. I. Title.
  QE862.S3P79 2012
  567.913—dc22

                          2010037186

First published in 2011 by
MACMILLAN EDUCATION AUSTRALIA PTY LTD
15–19 Claremont Street, South Yarra 3141

Visit our website at www.macmillan.com.au or go directly to www.macmillanlibrary.com.au

Associated companies and representatives throughout the world.

Copyright text © Kimberley Jane Pryor 2011

All rights reserved.

Publisher: Carmel Heron
Commissioning Editor: Niki Horin
Managing Editor: Vanessa Lanaway
Editor: Laura Jeanne Gobal
Proofreader: Helena Newton
Designer: Kerri Wilson (cover and text)
Page Layout: Pier Vido and Domenic Lauricella
Photo Researcher: Brendan Gallagher
Illustrator: Melissa Webb
Production Controller: Vanessa Johnson

Printed in China

Acknowledgments
The author and publisher are grateful to the following for permission to reproduce copyright material:

Photographs courtesy of: The Natural History Museum, London, **14**; Photolibrary/Brian Jaquest, **29**, /A B Joyce, **8**, / Joseph Nettis, **9**.

Background image of ripples on water © Shutterstock/ArchMan.

While every care has been taken to trace and acknowledge copyright, the publisher tenders their apologies for any accidental infringement where copyright has proved untraceable. They would be pleased to come to a suitable arrangement with the rightful owner in each case.

For Nick, Thomas, and Ashley

1 3 5 6 4 2

Contents

What Are Dinosaurs? 4

Dinosaur Groups 6

How Do We Know about Dinosaurs? 8

Meet Diplodocus 10

What Did Diplodocus Look Like? 12

The Skull and Senses of Diplodocus 14

Diplodocus Fossils 16

Where Did Diplodocus Live? 18

What Did Diplodocus Eat? 20

Predator or Prey? 22

How Did Diplodocus Live? 24

Life Cycle of Diplodocus 26

What Happened to Diplodocus? 28

Names and Their Meanings 30

Glossary 31

Index 32

When a word is printed in **bold**, you can look up its meaning in the glossary on page 31.

What Are Dinosaurs?

Dinosaurs (*dy-no-soars*) were **reptiles** that lived millions of years ago. They were different from other reptiles because their legs were directly under their bodies instead of to their sides like today's reptiles. Dinosaurs walked or ran on land.

At one time, there were more than 1,000 different kinds of dinosaurs.

Dinosaurs lived during a period of time called the Mesozoic (*mes-ah-zoh-ik*) Era. The Mesozoic Era is divided into the Triassic (*try-ass-ik*), Jurassic (*je-rass-ik*), and Cretaceous (*krah-tay-shahs*) periods.

This timeline shows the three different periods of the Mesozoic Era, when dinosaurs lived.

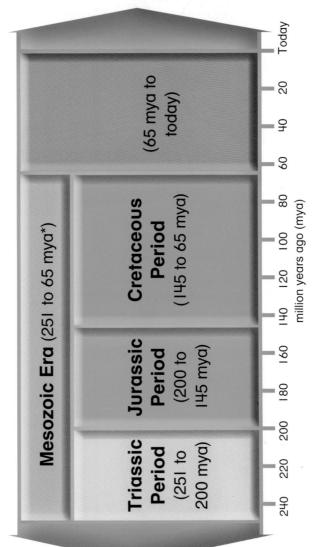

Mesozoic Era (251 to 65 mya*)

Triassic Period
(251 to 200 mya)

Jurassic Period
(200 to 145 mya)

Cretaceous Period
(145 to 65 mya)

(65 mya to today)

240 220 200 180 160 140 120 100 80 60 40 20 Today

million years ago (mya)

*Note: mya = million years ago

Dinosaur Groups

Dinosaurs are sorted into two main groups according to their hipbones. Some dinosaurs had hipbones like a lizard's. Other dinosaurs had hipbones like a bird's.

All dinosaurs were either lizard-hipped or bird-hipped.

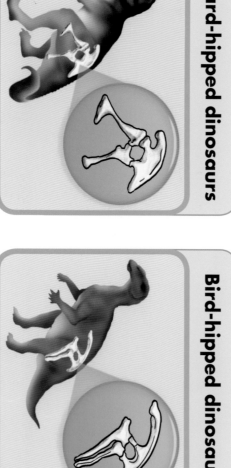

Dinosaurs

Lizard-hipped dinosaurs

Bird-hipped dinosaurs

Dinosaurs can be sorted into five smaller groups. Some lizard-hipped dinosaurs walked on two legs and ate meat. Others walked on four legs and ate plants. All bird-hipped dinosaurs ate plants.

Main Group	Smaller Group	Features	Examples
Lizard-hipped	Theropoda (*ther-ah-poh-dah*)	• Small to large • Walked on two legs • Meat-eaters	Tyrannosaurus Velociraptor
	Sauropodomorpha (*soar-rop-ah-dah-mor-fah*)	• Huge • Walked on four legs • Plant-eaters	Diplodocus
Bird-hipped	Thyreophora (*theer-ee-off-or-ah*)	• Small to large • Walked on four legs • Plant-eaters	Ankylosaurus
	Ornithopoda (*or-ni-thop-oh-dah*)	• Small to large • Walked on two or four legs • Plant-eaters	Muttaburrasaurus
	Ceratopsia (*ser-ah-top-see-ah*)	• Small to large • Walked on two or four legs • Plant-eaters • Frilled and horned skulls	Protoceratops

This table shows how dinosaurs can be sorted according to their size, how they walked, and the food they ate.

How Do We Know about Dinosaurs?

We know about dinosaurs because people have found fossils. Fossils are the preserved remains of plants and animals that lived long ago. They include bones, teeth, footprints, and eggs.

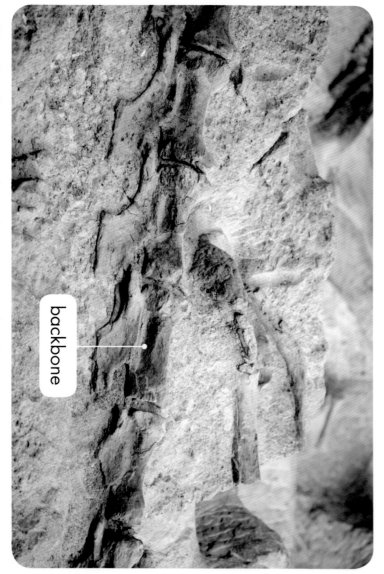

backbone

This fossil is part of the backbone of a Diplodocus.

People who study fossils are called paleontologists (*pail-ee-on-tol-oh-jists*). They study fossils to learn about dinosaurs. They also remove dinosaur bones from rocks and rebuild **skeletons.**

fossils

Paleontologists study fossils in dinosaur workrooms.

Meet Diplodocus

Diplodocus (*di-plo-doh-kuss*) was a huge, lizard-hipped dinosaur. It belonged to a group of dinosaurs called sauropodomorpha. Dinosaurs in this group walked on four legs and ate plants.

Diplodocus had a very long neck!

Diplodocus lived in the late Jurassic period, between 150 and 145 million years ago.

The purple area on this timeline shows when Diplodocus lived.

Mesozoic Era (251 to 65 mya*)

Triassic Period (251 to 200 mya)

Jurassic Period (200 to 145 mya)

Cretaceous Period (145 to 65 mya)

(65 mya to today)

240 220 200 180 160 140 120 100 80 60 40 20 Today

million years ago (mya)

When Diplodocus lived

*Note: mya = million years ago

What Did Diplodocus Look Like?

Diplodocus was 89 feet (27 meters) long and 16 feet (5 meters) tall at the hips. It weighed 12 tons (11 tonnes).

Diplodocus was as long as two school buses and heavier than two elephants!

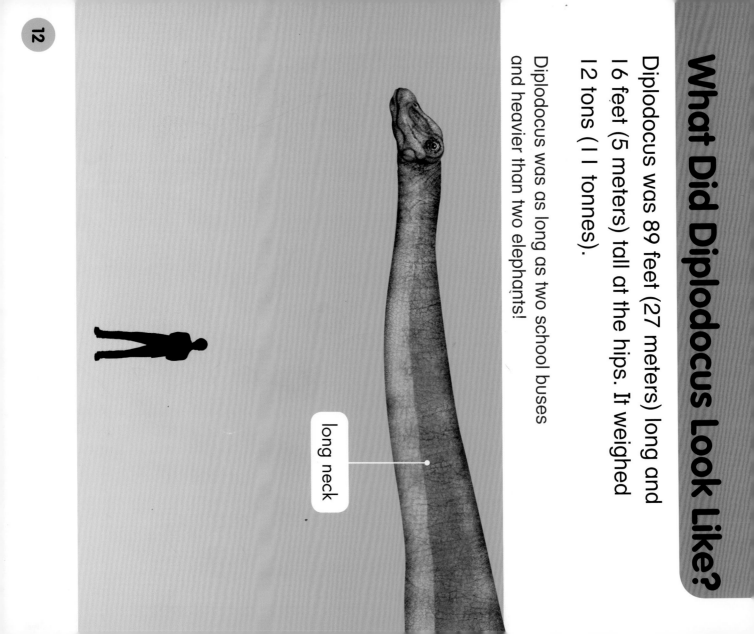

long neck

Diplodocus walked on four legs. It had a long neck and a whiplike tail. Diplodocus had small bumps on its skin.

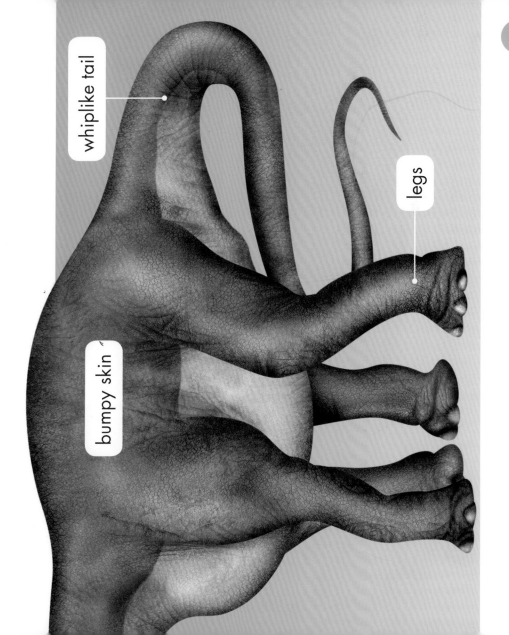

whiplike tail

legs

bumpy skin

The Skull and Senses of Diplodocus

Diplodocus had a tiny skull and brain. This meant that it was one of the least smart dinosaurs!

Diplodocus had thin, pencil-like teeth in the front of its mouth.

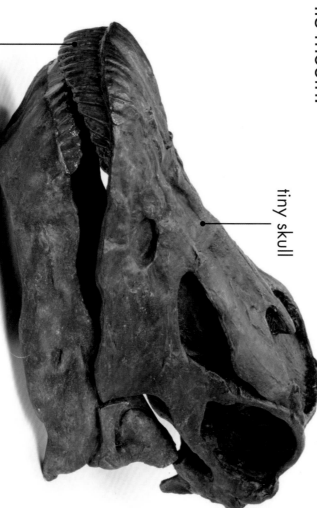

tiny skull

thin, pencil-like teeth

An adult Diplodocus skull had a long, square snout.

Diplodocus had eyes on the sides of its head. This helped it to see a lot of its surroundings but did not help Diplodocus see things in front of it. Diplodocus probably had a fair **sense** of smell.

The Senses of Diplodocus

Sense	Very Good	Good	Fair	Unable to Say
Sight			✓	
Hearing			✓	
Smell			✓	
Taste				✓
Touch				✓

Diplodocus Fossils

Diplodocus fossils have been found in the United States.

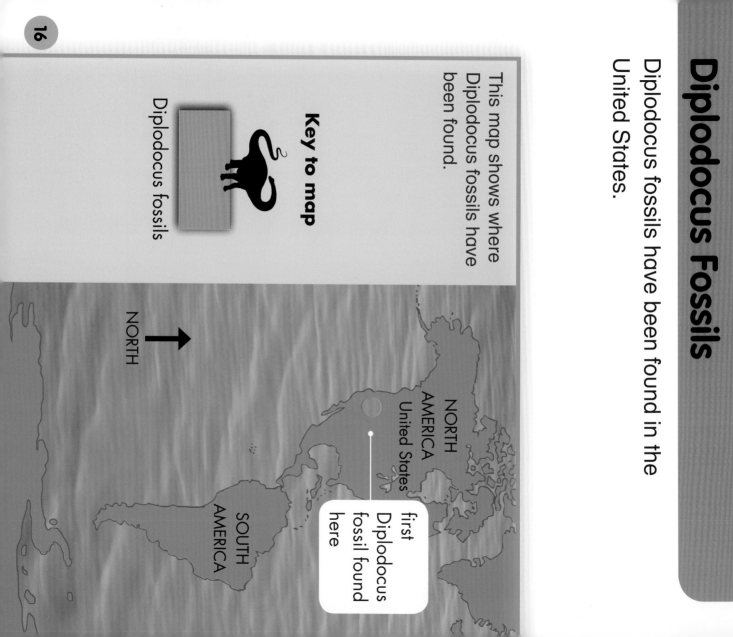

This map shows where Diplodocus fossils have been found.

Key to map

Diplodocus fossils

NORTH

NORTH AMERICA
United States

first Diplodocus fossil found here

SOUTH AMERICA

In 1878, paleontologists Benjamin Mudge and Samuel Wendell Williston found the first Diplodocus fossil in Wyoming. It was an entire skeleton. More fossils have been found since then.

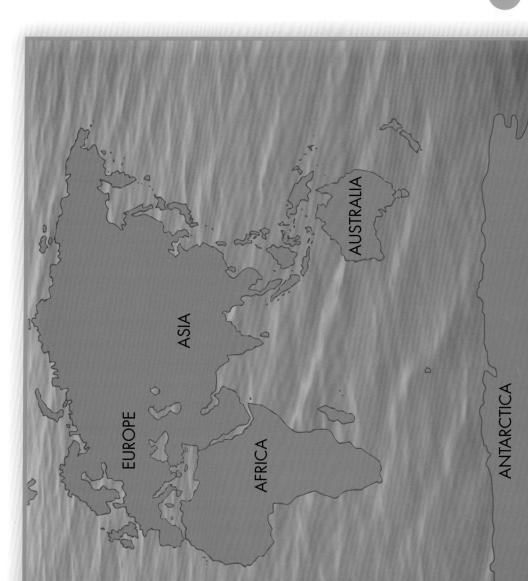

Where Did Diplodocus Live?

Diplodocus lived on **plains**. These plains had groups of small- and medium-sized plants. Forest trees such as ginkgos and conifers could be found on the edges of the plains.

horsetails

ginkgos

The plains where Diplodocus lived had different kinds of plants. These included cycads, ferns, horsetails, and club moss.

Diplodocus was so huge that it had to live in open areas of land.

ferns

conifers

cycads

club moss

What Did Diplodocus Eat?

Diplodocus was a herbivore, or plant-eater. It stripped soft leaves from plants with its thin teeth.

Foods Eaten by Diplodocus

Conifers	
Club Moss	
Ferns	
Horsetails	

Diplodocus fed on plants as it walked across the plains. It could swallow leaves whole. Some paleontologists think Diplodocus swallowed stones to help it grind up the leaves in its stomach!

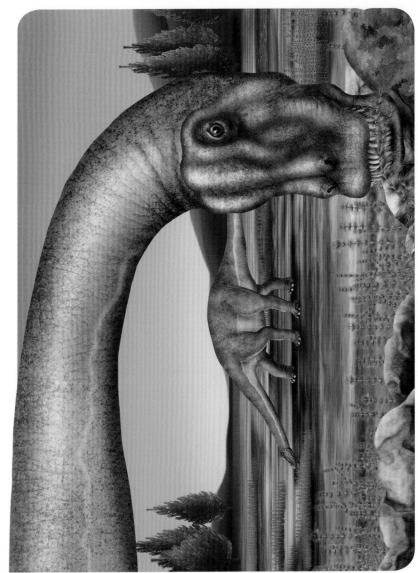

Diplodocus could reach its food by moving its neck to the side.

Predator or Prey?

Diplodocus was **prey** for a meat-eating dinosaur called Allosaurus (*al-oh-soar-us*). This large and scary **predator** often attacked young Diplodocuses.

A young Diplodocus would have been too small to defend itself against an adult Allosaurus.

Diplodocus was a huge dinosaur. Its size was its main defense against predators. It also protected itself by living in a herd, or group.

Diplodocus may have cracked its huge tail like a whip to defend itself against predators.

How Did Diplodocus Live?

Paleontologists think Diplodocus lived in a herd because they have found lines of footprints. These footprints were made by dinosaurs similar to Diplodocus that were traveling in a herd.

A line of dinosaur footprints is known as a trackway.

Paleontologists think Diplodocus spent most of its time eating because it had a tiny mouth. A tiny mouth can chew only a tiny amount of food at a time.

The amount of plants Diplodocus ate daily may have weighed as much as a car!

Life Cycle of Diplodocus

Paleontologists study fossils and living animals to learn about the life cycle of Diplodocus.

1. An adult male Diplodocus displayed his long neck to attract a female. The male and female **mated**.

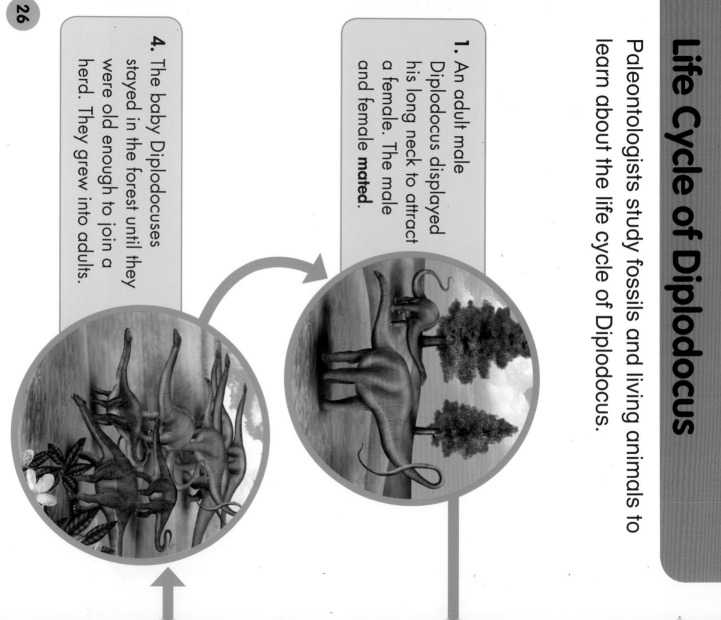

4. The baby Diplodocuses stayed in the forest until they were old enough to join a herd. They grew into adults.

They believe there were four main stages in the life cycle of Diplodocus. This is what it may have been like.

2. The female laid eggs in an open area at the edge of a forest while walking. She did not care for or guard her eggs.

3. Baby Diplodocuses hatched from the eggs. They walked deep into the forest so they could find food and hide from predators.

What Happened to Diplodocus?

Diplodocus became **extinct** about 145 million years ago. Some paleontologists think Diplodocus died out because the herds trampled on or ate all the plants.

Large herds of Diplodocuses may have destroyed all of the plants.

The last dinosaurs became extinct about 65 million years ago. Many paleontologists think dinosaurs died out when a large **meteorite** hit Earth. Others think **climate change** or volcanoes caused their extinction.

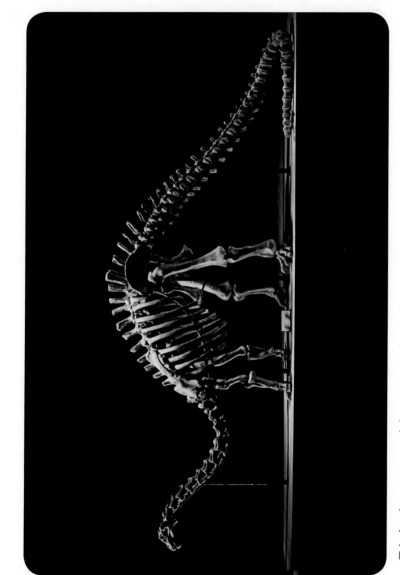

Diplodocus could not survive changing conditions on Earth, leaving us with only fossils.

Names and Their Meanings

Dinosaurs are named by people who discover them or paleontologists who study them. A dinosaur may be named for its appearance or behavior. Its name may also honor a person or place.

Name	Meaning
Dinosaur	Terrible lizard—because people thought dinosaurs were powerful lizards
Ankylosaurus	Fused lizard—because many of its bones were joined together
Diplodocus	Double beam—because it had special bones in its tail
Muttaburrasaurus	Muttaburra lizard—because it was discovered near the town of Muttaburra, in Australia
Protoceratops	First horned face—because it was one of the early horned dinosaurs
Tyrannosaurus	Tyrant lizard—because it was a fearsome ruler of the land
Velociraptor	Speedy thief—because it ran quickly and ate meat

Glossary

climate change   Changes in the usual weather in a place.

extinct   No longer existing.

mated   Created offspring.

meteorite   A rock from space that has landed on Earth.

plains   Wide, flat areas of land.

predator   An animal that hunts and kills other animals for food.

prey   An animal that is hunted and killed by other animals for food.

reptiles   Creeping or crawling animals that are covered with scales.

sense   A special ability that people and animals use to experience the world around them. Typically, those senses are sight, hearing, smell, taste, and touch.

skeletons   The bones inside the body of a person or an animal.

Index

B
bird-hipped dinosaurs, 6, 7
brain, 14

C
Cretaceous period, 5, 11

E
eggs, 8, 27
extinction, 28, 29

F
food, 7, 20, 21, 25, 27, 28
fossils, 8, 9, 16–17, 26, 29

H
herbivores, 20

J
Jurassic period, 5, 11

L
life cycle, 26–27
lizard-hipped dinosaurs, 6, 7,
   10

M
meat-eating dinosaurs, 7, 22,
   30

Mesozoic Era, 5, 11

N
neck, 12, 13, 21, 26

P
paleontologists, 9, 17, 21, 24,
   25, 26, 28, 29, 30
plains, 18, 19, 21
plant-eating dinosaurs, 7, 10,
   20, 21, 25, 28
predators, 22, 23, 27
prey, 22

R
reptiles, 4

S
senses, 15
skeletons, 9, 17
skin, 13
skulls, 7, 14

T
tail, 13, 23, 30
teeth, 8, 14, 20
Triassic period, 5, 11